# One Hundred
## Ways to Get to
# 100

by Jerry Pallotta

Illustrated by Rob Bolster

SCHOLASTIC INC.

New York   Toronto   London   Auckland   Sydney   Mexico City   New Delhi   Hong Kong   Buenos Aires

*One hundred hugs and kisses to Gina Mazzola.*
*—Jerry Pallotta*

*This book is dedicated to Tom Sgouros, former head of the illustration department at R.I.S.D.,*
*who taught me that less is sometimes better than more.*
*—Rob Bolster*

Library of Congress Cataloging-in-Publication Data available.

ISBN 0-439-38913-5

12                                                    08

Printed in the U.S.A.
First printing, January 2003

If you can count to ten, you can count to one hundred.
One, two, three, four, five, six, seven, eight, nine, ten.

# Count by Ones

1　2　3　4　5　6　7　8　9　10

11　12　13　14　15　16　17　18　19　20

21　22　23　24　25　26　27　28　29　30

31　32　33　34　35　36　37　38　39　40

41　42　43　44　45　46　47　48　49　50

Keep on counting . . . eleven, twelve, thirteen, fourteen, fifteen, sixteen, seventeen, eighteen, nineteen, twenty, twenty-one, twenty-two, twenty-three, twenty-four, twenty-five, twenty-six, twenty-seven, twenty-eight, twenty-nine, thirty, and keep on going . . .

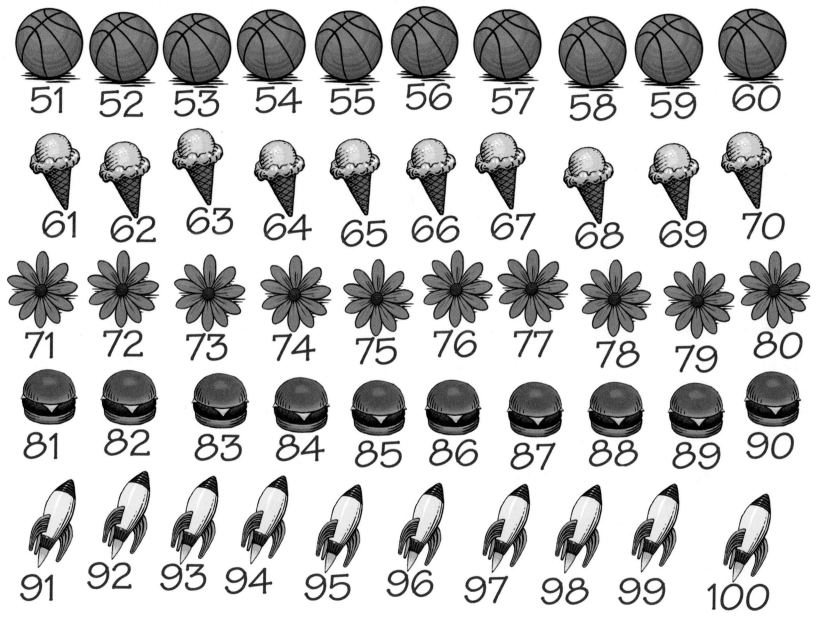

51 52 53 54 55 56 57 58 59 60

61 62 63 64 65 66 67 68 69 70

71 72 73 74 75 76 77 78 79 80

81 82 83 84 85 86 87 88 89 90

91 92 93 94 95 96 97 98 99 100

You're almost there! Eighty-eight, eighty-nine, ninety, ninety-one,
ninety-two, ninety-three, ninety-four, ninety-five, ninety-six, ninety-seven . . .
Keep on counting, you're getting close, ninety-eight, ninety-nine, ONE HUNDRED!
There is a number for every item you count.

# Twos

2  4  6  8  10  12  14  16  18  20

22  24  26  28  30  32  34  36  38  40

42  44  46  48  50  52  54  56  58  60

62  64  66  68  70  72  74  76  78  80

82  84  86  88  90  92  94  96  98  100

Counting by ones took a long time. This time, count by twos. Do you know any twins? Think of these red cherries as twins. Two, four, six, eight, ten, twelve, fourteen, sixteen, eighteen, twenty, twenty-two, twenty-four, twenty-six . . . You do it! Skip count by twos all the way to ONE HUNDRED!

# Fours

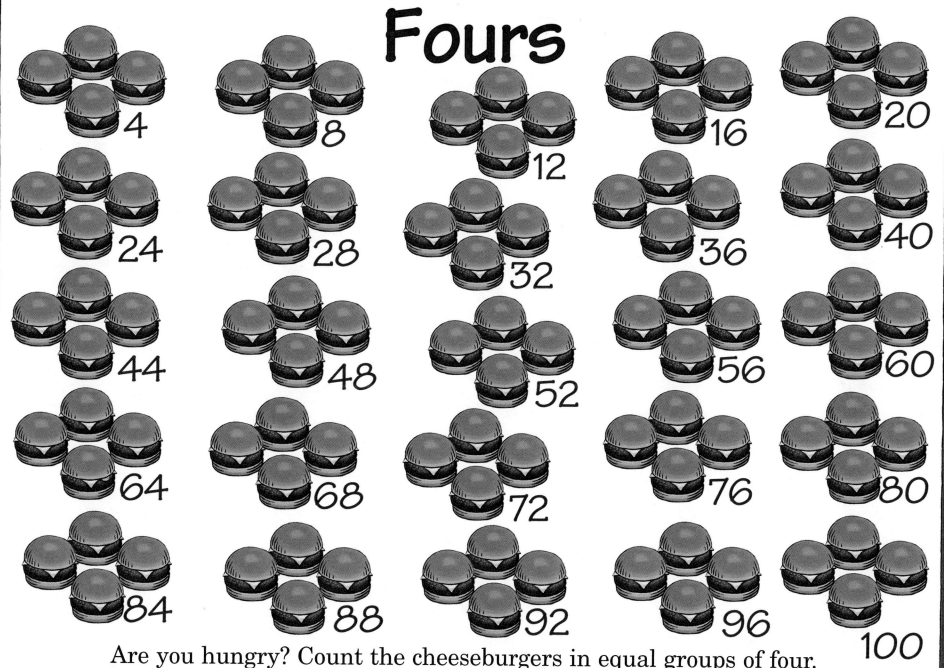

4
8
12
16
20
24
28
32
36
40
44
48
52
56
60
64
68
72
76
80
84
88
92
96
100

Are you hungry? Count the cheeseburgers in equal groups of four.
Four, eight, twelve, sixteen, twenty, twenty-four, twenty-eight, thirty-two,
thirty-six, forty, forty-four, forty-eight, fifty-two, fifty-six, sixty, sixty-four,
sixty-eight, seventy-two, seventy-six, eighty, eighty-four, eighty-eight,
ninety-two, ninety-six, ONE HUNDRED! Find the one with pickles.

# Fives

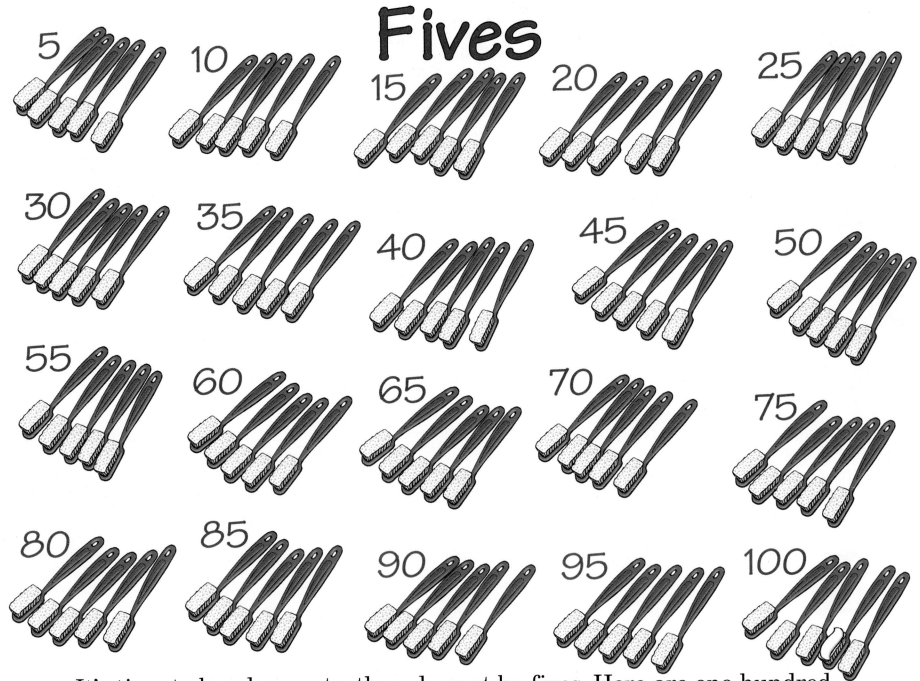

It's time to brush your teeth and count by fives. Here are one hundred toothbrushes: five, ten, fifteen, twenty, twenty-five, thirty, thirty-five, forty, forty-five, fifty, fifty-five, sixty, sixty-five, seventy, seventy-five, eighty, eighty-five ninety, ninety-five, ONE HUNDRED! Where is the one with toothpaste?

# Tens

10 20 30 40 50 60 70 80 90 100

Do not count these one hundred fish one at a time.
Count by tens! Ten fish, twenty fish, thirty fish, forty fish, fifty fish,
sixty fish, seventy fish, eighty fish, ninety fish, ONE HUNDRED fish!
Now try it fast. It's a tongue twister.

# Twenties

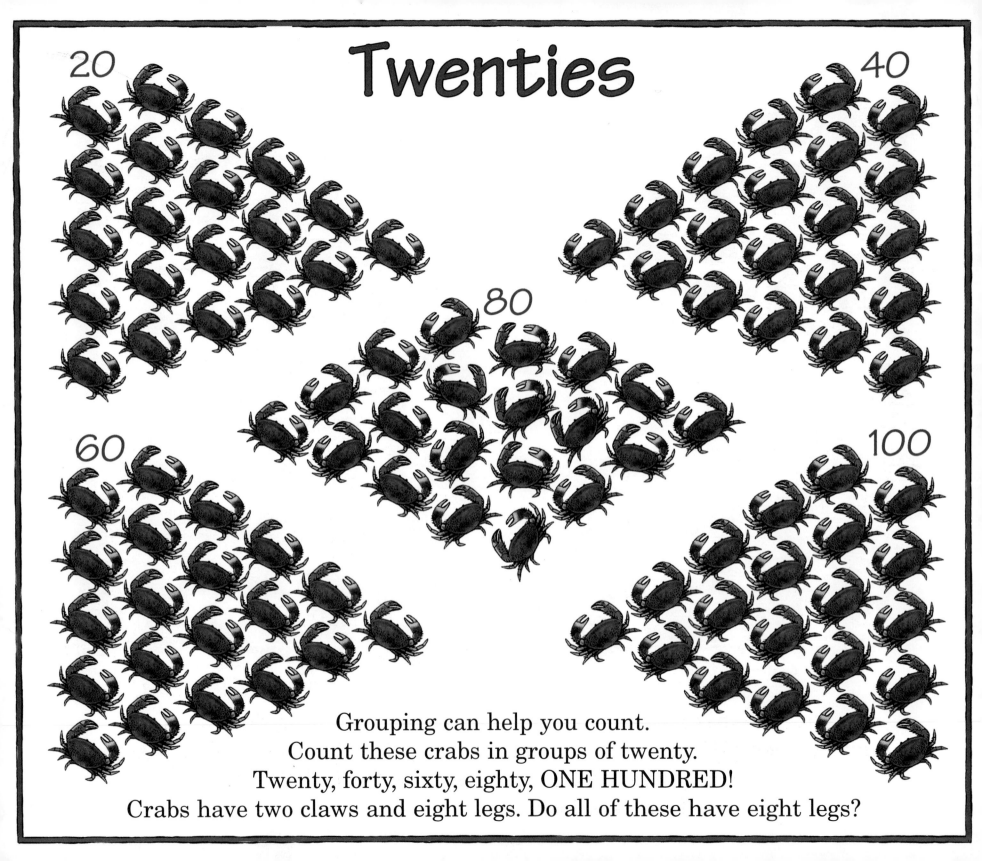

20

40

80

60

100

Grouping can help you count.
Count these crabs in groups of twenty.
Twenty, forty, sixty, eighty, ONE HUNDRED!
Crabs have two claws and eight legs. Do all of these have eight legs?

# Twenty-fives

Pretend it is millions of years ago. You are counting dinosaurs.
Count by twenty-fives. You must count quickly. The dinosaurs might see you.
Twenty-five, fifty, seventy-five, ONE HUNDRED!
There are four groups of twenty-five.

# Fifties

50

100

Here are two groups of fifty rockets. Just count: fifty, ONE HUNDRED!
You could say fifty times two equals one hundred.

$1 \times 100 = 100$   turtles and other items one at a time

$2 \times 50 = 100$   twin red cherries in fifty groups

$4 \times 25 = 100$   four cheeseburgers in twenty-five groups

$5 \times 20 = 100$   five toothbrushes in twenty groups

$10 \times 10 = 100$   ten fish in ten schools

$20 \times 5 = 100$   twenty crabs in five groups

$25 \times 4 = 100$   twenty-five dinosaurs in four groups

$50 \times 2 = 100$   fifty rockets in two groups

$100 \times 1 = 100$   ONE HUNDRED butterflies coming soon

We counted by ones, we counted by equal groups. Counting by equal groups is really multiplication. You did simple multiplication and you didn't even know it!

# 100+0=100

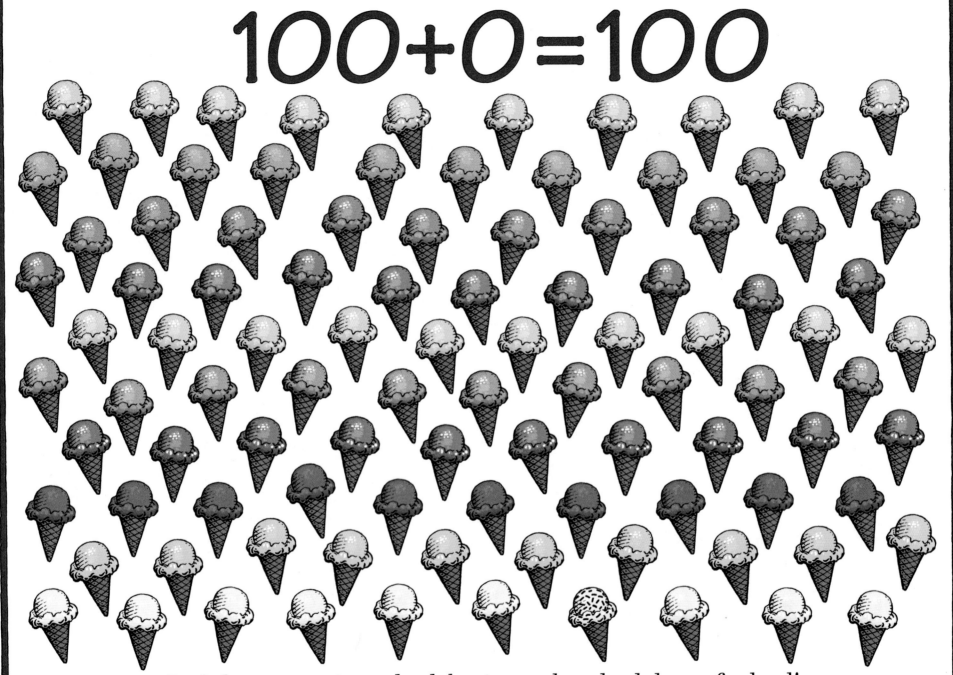

Let's have a party and celebrate one hundred days of school!
You can use addition to get to one hundred. Add zero.
One hundred ice-cream cones plus zero ice-cream cones still equals ONE HUNDRED
ice-cream cones. Zero has no value. Nothing has changed by adding a zero.

# 99+1=100

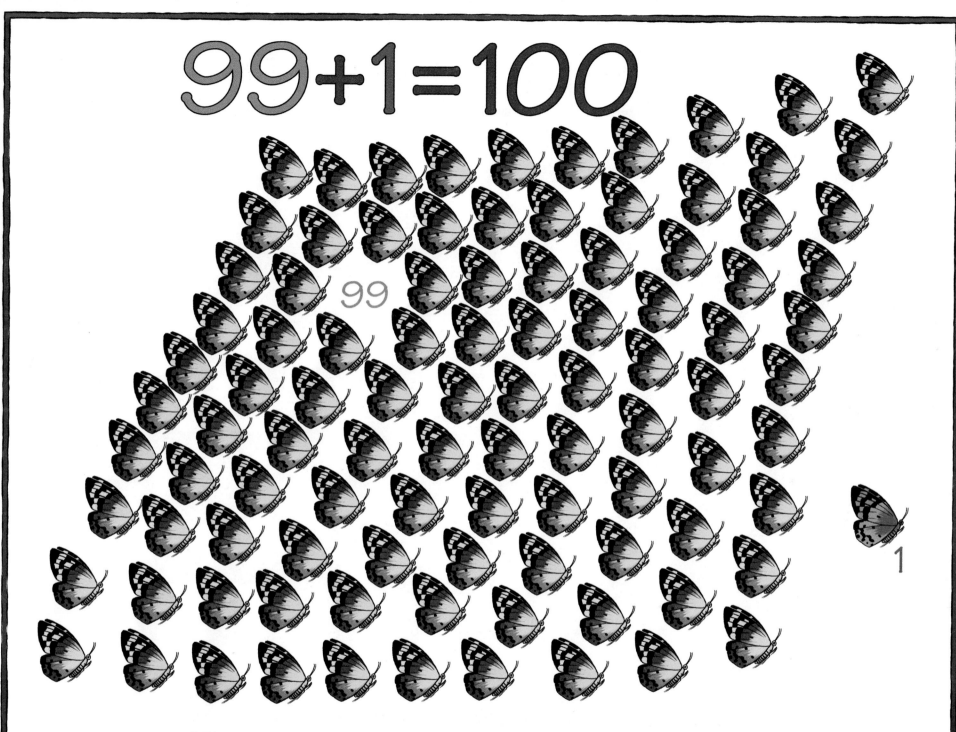

99

1

Ninety-nine orange butterflies plus one blue butterfly
equals ONE HUNDRED butterflies. One is a single-digit number.
Ninety-nine is a two-digit number. One hundred is a three-digit number.

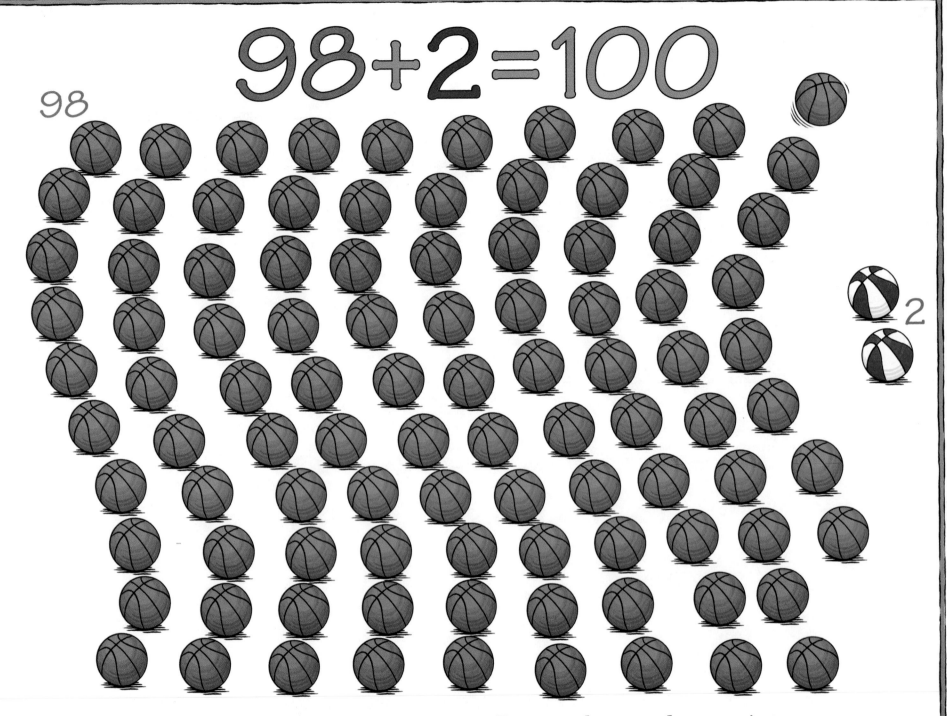

Don't dribble. Don't throw a pass. Do not shoot a three-pointer.
Take a time-out and add these basketballs. Ninety-eight basketballs plus
two basketballs equals ONE HUNDRED basketballs. Nice job, take a free throw!

# 97+3=100

97

3

Here are pencils. If we make mistakes, we can use the erasers.
Ninety-seven plus three equals ONE HUNDRED. These addition equations
have a pattern. The first number keeps getting smaller by one,
and the second number keeps getting larger by one.

# 32+68=100

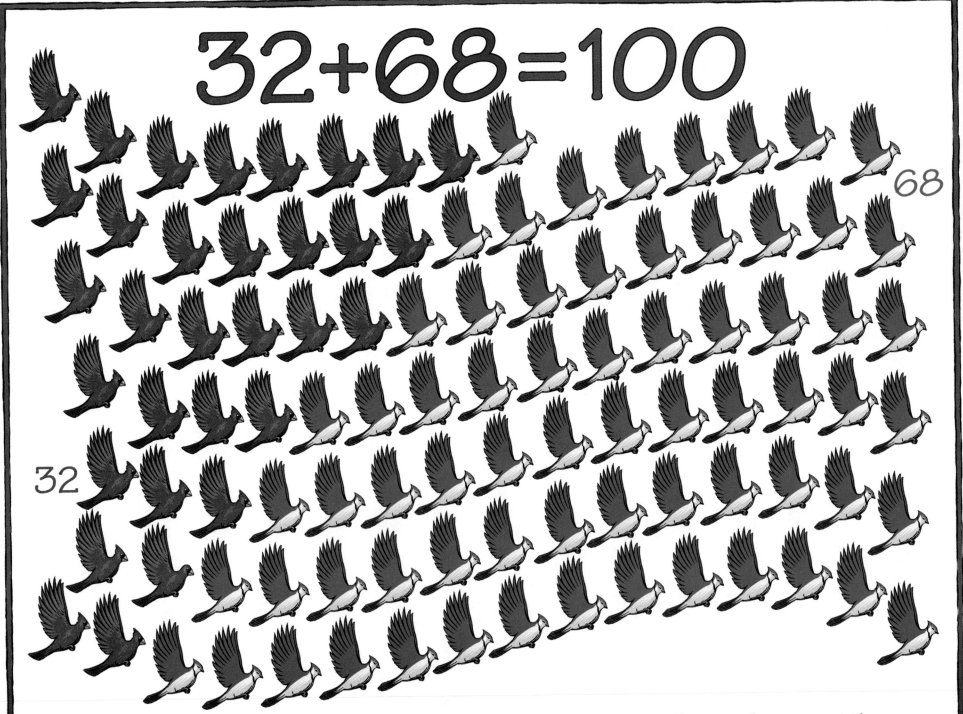

96+4=100 is the next logical equation, but here is a totally random equation. Thirty-two cardinals plus sixty-eight blue jays equals ONE HUNDRED birds. Bird-watching is fun. Which one is missing feathers?

# 81+19=100

If these frogs stop jumping, we can count them. Eighty-one purple frogs plus nineteen yellow frogs equals ONE HUNDRED really cool frogs.

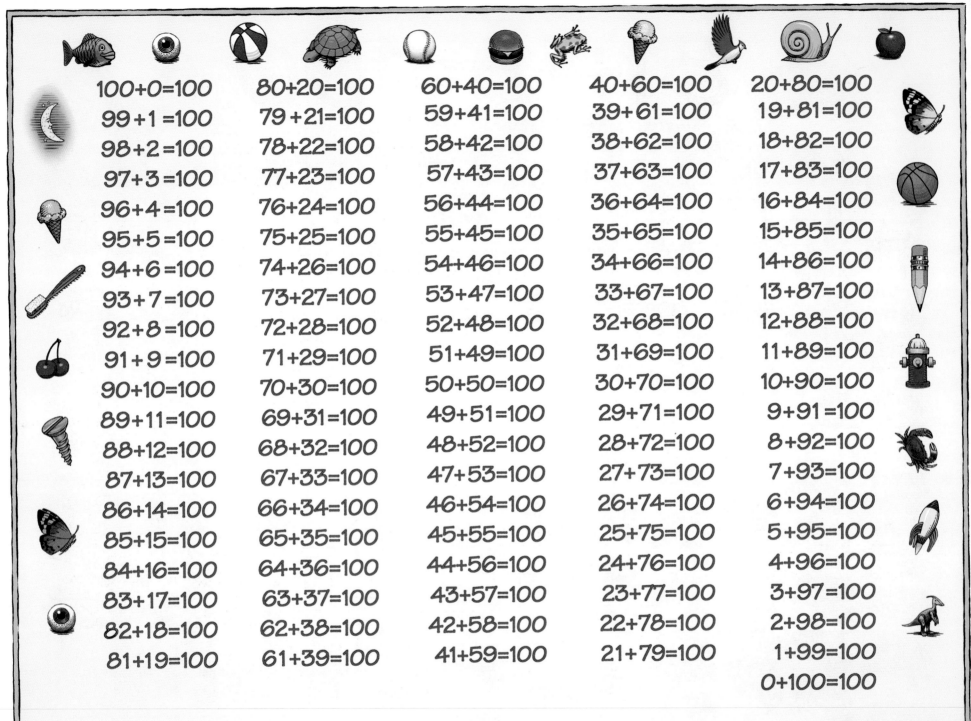

| | | | | |
|---|---|---|---|---|
| 100+0=100 | 80+20=100 | 60+40=100 | 40+60=100 | 20+80=100 |
| 99+1=100 | 79+21=100 | 59+41=100 | 39+61=100 | 19+81=100 |
| 98+2=100 | 78+22=100 | 58+42=100 | 38+62=100 | 18+82=100 |
| 97+3=100 | 77+23=100 | 57+43=100 | 37+63=100 | 17+83=100 |
| 96+4=100 | 76+24=100 | 56+44=100 | 36+64=100 | 16+84=100 |
| 95+5=100 | 75+25=100 | 55+45=100 | 35+65=100 | 15+85=100 |
| 94+6=100 | 74+26=100 | 54+46=100 | 34+66=100 | 14+86=100 |
| 93+7=100 | 73+27=100 | 53+47=100 | 33+67=100 | 13+87=100 |
| 92+8=100 | 72+28=100 | 52+48=100 | 32+68=100 | 12+88=100 |
| 91+9=100 | 71+29=100 | 51+49=100 | 31+69=100 | 11+89=100 |
| 90+10=100 | 70+30=100 | 50+50=100 | 30+70=100 | 10+90=100 |
| 89+11=100 | 69+31=100 | 49+51=100 | 29+71=100 | 9+91=100 |
| 88+12=100 | 68+32=100 | 48+52=100 | 28+72=100 | 8+92=100 |
| 87+13=100 | 67+33=100 | 47+53=100 | 27+73=100 | 7+93=100 |
| 86+14=100 | 66+34=100 | 46+54=100 | 26+74=100 | 6+94=100 |
| 85+15=100 | 65+35=100 | 45+55=100 | 25+75=100 | 5+95=100 |
| 84+16=100 | 64+36=100 | 44+56=100 | 24+76=100 | 4+96=100 |
| 83+17=100 | 63+37=100 | 43+57=100 | 23+77=100 | 3+97=100 |
| 82+18=100 | 62+38=100 | 42+58=100 | 22+78=100 | 2+98=100 |
| 81+19=100 | 61+39=100 | 41+59=100 | 21+79=100 | 1+99=100 |
| | | | | 0+100=100 |

Did you doubt that there are one hundred ways to count to one hundred?
On this page alone there are one hundred and one ways. This is a summary
of addition equations using two whole numbers to get to ONE HUNDRED!

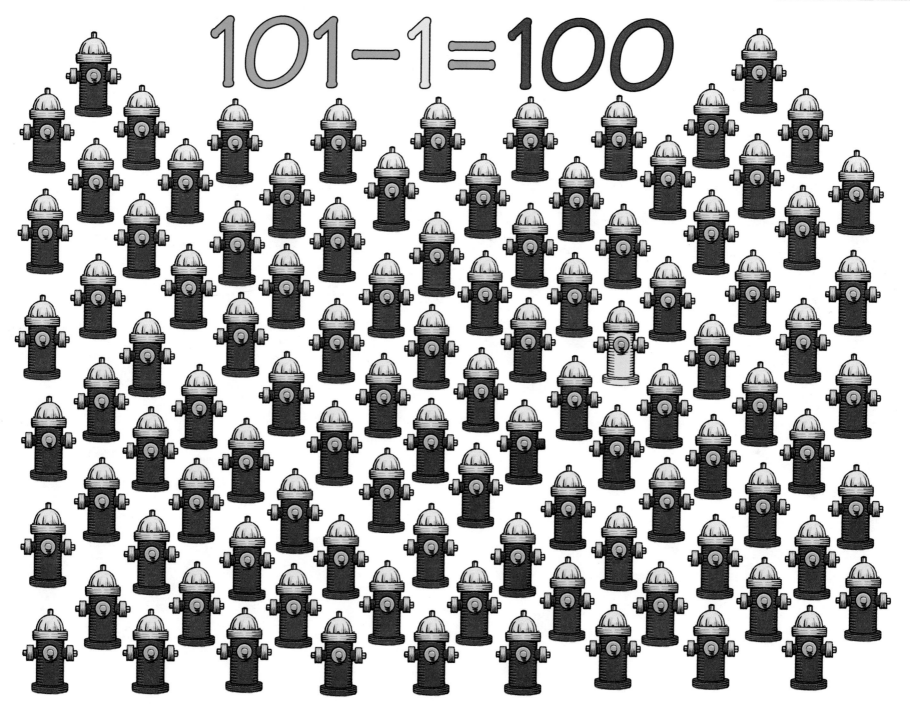

# 101−1=100

Let's subtract our way to one hundred. Subtraction is taking away
or finding the difference. Here are one hundred and one fire hydrants.
Take the yellow one away. You now have ONE HUNDRED red fire hydrants.

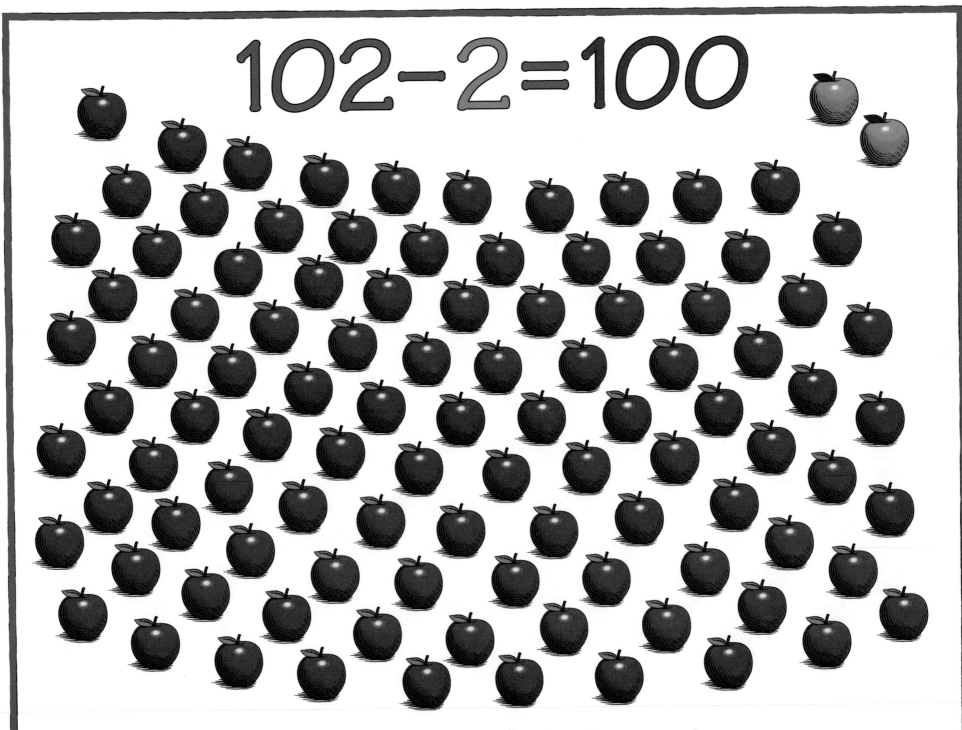

# 102-2=100

Let's start with one hundred and two apples.
Eat the two green ones. You now have ONE HUNDRED red apples left over.
This is another example of "take away" subtraction.

# 103-3=100

There were one hundred and three green turtles on this page. Three green turtles got erased. One hundred and three green turtles minus three green turtles equals ONE HUNDRED green turtles!

# 104-4=100

Here is some "comparison" subtraction. On this page are one hundred and four screws. Find the difference. One hundred and four screws minus four steel screws equals ONE HUNDRED brass screws. Try to find the Phillips head screw.

# 200-100=100

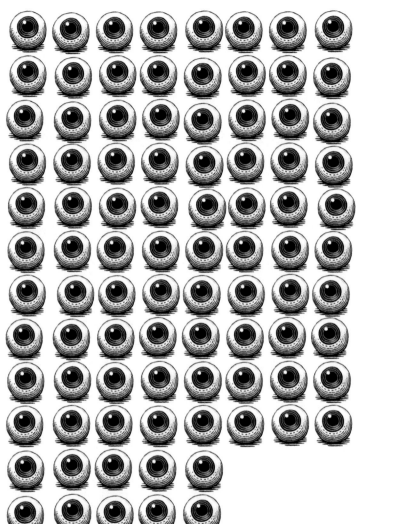

This is a spooky page.
Two hundred eyeballs are looking
at you. There are two groups.
One hundred eyeballs are blue.
One hundred eyeballs are brown. Take one group away.
Two hundred minus one hundred equals ONE HUNDRED!

# 1000-900=100

One thousand is a four digit number.

This time, do not count the flowers. Count the one thousand petals.

Take away nine hundred colorful petals. One hundred white petals are left over.

One thousand minus nine hundred equals ONE HUNDRED. Subtraction is fun!

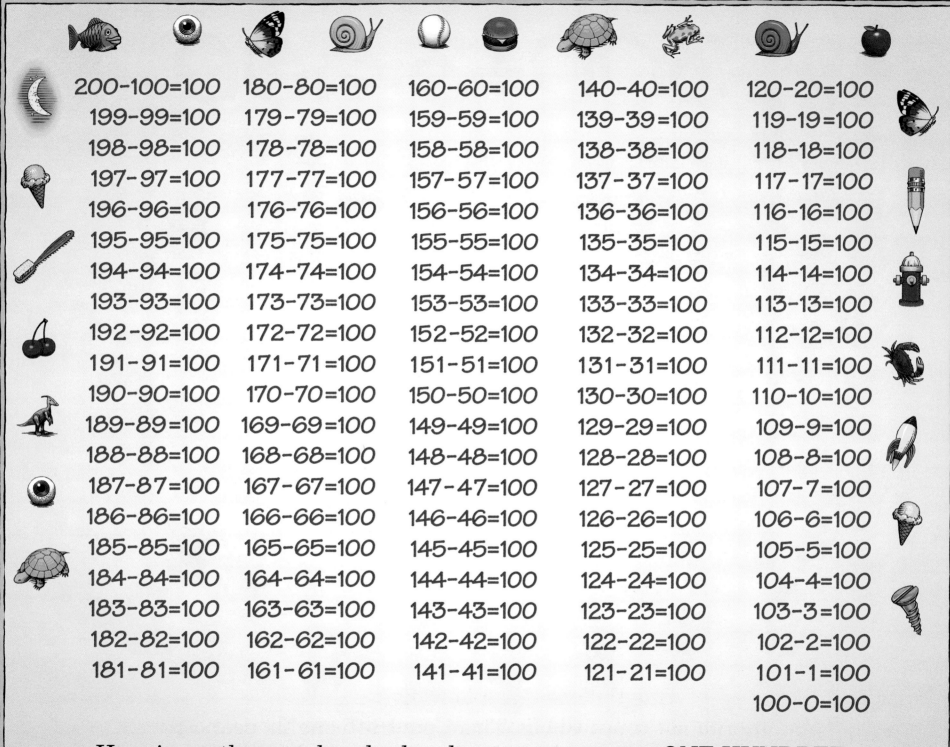

| | | | | |
|---|---|---|---|---|
| 200-100=100 | 180-80=100 | 160-60=100 | 140-40=100 | 120-20=100 |
| 199-99=100 | 179-79=100 | 159-59=100 | 139-39=100 | 119-19=100 |
| 198-98=100 | 178-78=100 | 158-58=100 | 138-38=100 | 118-18=100 |
| 197-97=100 | 177-77=100 | 157-57=100 | 137-37=100 | 117-17=100 |
| 196-96=100 | 176-76=100 | 156-56=100 | 136-36=100 | 116-16=100 |
| 195-95=100 | 175-75=100 | 155-55=100 | 135-35=100 | 115-15=100 |
| 194-94=100 | 174-74=100 | 154-54=100 | 134-34=100 | 114-14=100 |
| 193-93=100 | 173-73=100 | 153-53=100 | 133-33=100 | 113-13=100 |
| 192-92=100 | 172-72=100 | 152-52=100 | 132-32=100 | 112-12=100 |
| 191-91=100 | 171-71=100 | 151-51=100 | 131-31=100 | 111-11=100 |
| 190-90=100 | 170-70=100 | 150-50=100 | 130-30=100 | 110-10=100 |
| 189-89=100 | 169-69=100 | 149-49=100 | 129-29=100 | 109-9=100 |
| 188-88=100 | 168-68=100 | 148-48=100 | 128-28=100 | 108-8=100 |
| 187-87=100 | 167-67=100 | 147-47=100 | 127-27=100 | 107-7=100 |
| 186-86=100 | 166-66=100 | 146-46=100 | 126-26=100 | 106-6=100 |
| 185-85=100 | 165-65=100 | 145-45=100 | 125-25=100 | 105-5=100 |
| 184-84=100 | 164-64=100 | 144-44=100 | 124-24=100 | 104-4=100 |
| 183-83=100 | 163-63=100 | 143-43=100 | 123-23=100 | 103-3=100 |
| 182-82=100 | 162-62=100 | 142-42=100 | 122-22=100 | 102-2=100 |
| 181-81=100 | 161-61=100 | 141-41=100 | 121-21=100 | 101-1=100 |
| | | | | 100-0=100 |

Here is another one hundred and one ways to get to ONE HUNDRED.
This subtraction summary did not have to end. It could go on forever.

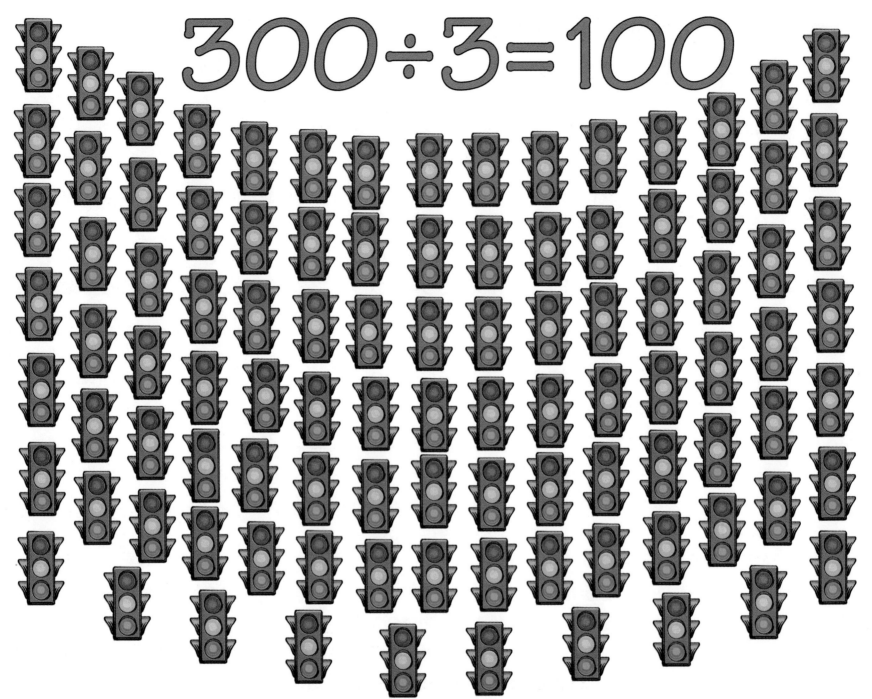

# 300÷3=100

You are riding the school bus. There are traffic lights everywhere.
Group these three hundred lights by color. Green . . . yellow . . . red! Stop! *300÷3=100*.
There are ONE HUNDRED traffic signals. We got to one hundred by using division.

# 200 ÷ 2 = 100

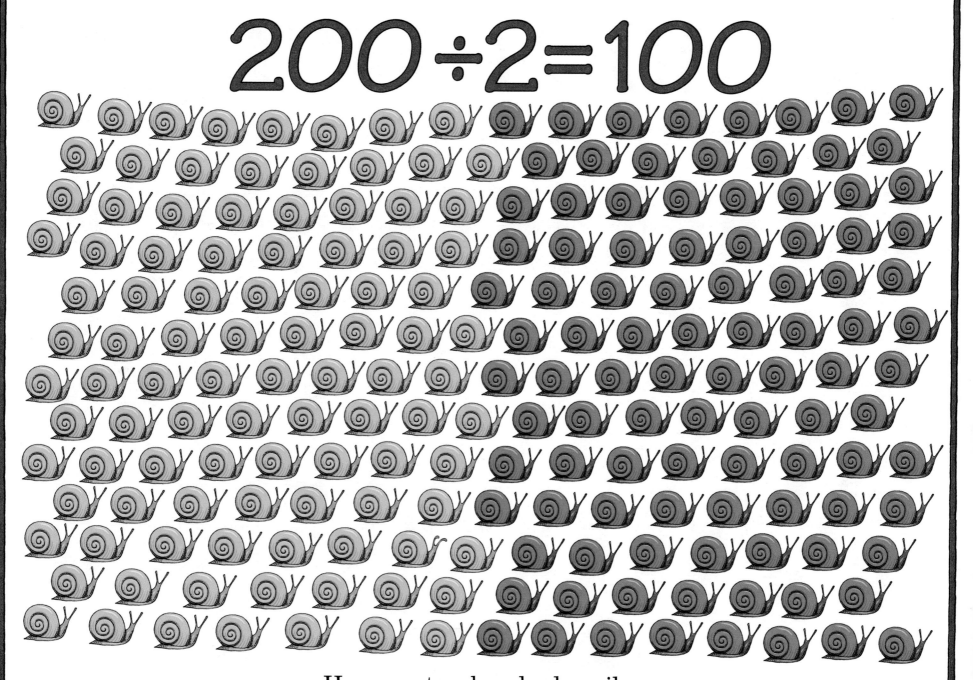

Here are two hundred snails.
Use division! Divide the snails into two equal groups.
Two hundred divided by two equals ONE HUNDRED.
One of the snails is tired. Can you find it?

# 100÷1=100

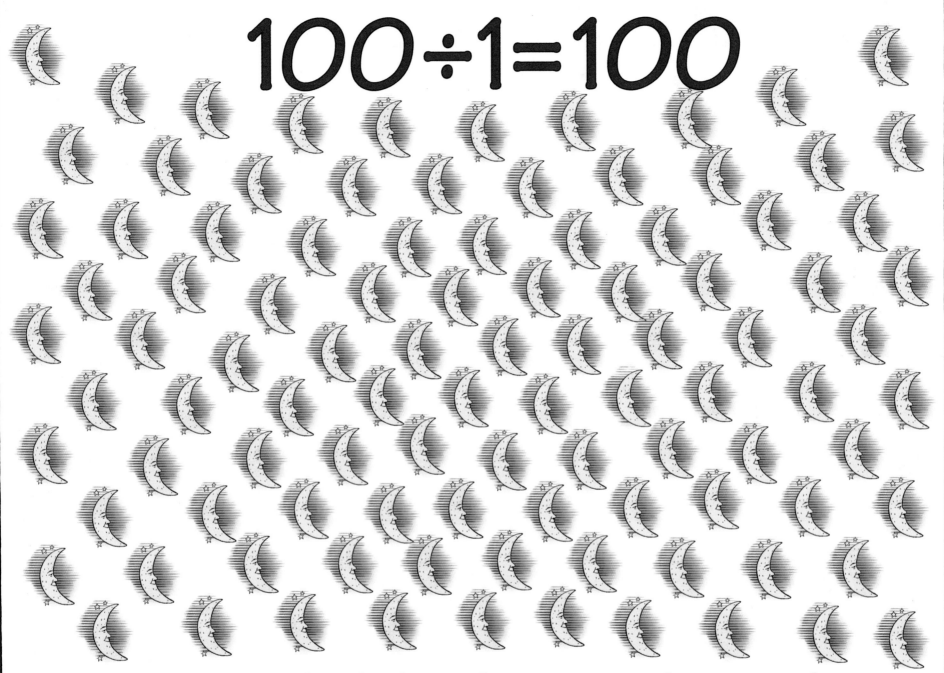

If you divide something by the number one, you get the same number. One hundred divided by one equals ONE HUNDRED. You could look at this page as one moon one hundred times or one group of one hundred moons. Be a math star! Find the moon that is different.

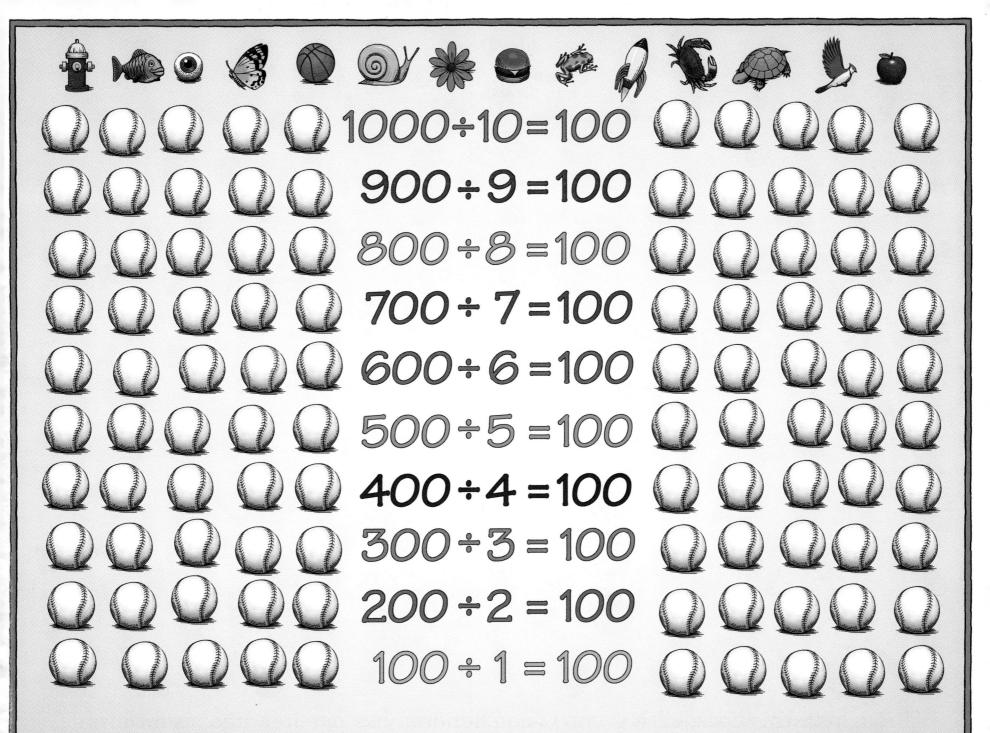

$$1000 \div 10 = 100$$

$$900 \div 9 = 100$$

$$800 \div 8 = 100$$

$$700 \div 7 = 100$$

$$600 \div 6 = 100$$

$$500 \div 5 = 100$$

$$400 \div 4 = 100$$

$$300 \div 3 = 100$$

$$200 \div 2 = 100$$

$$100 \div 1 = 100$$

Dividing a number into equal amounts is called division. It is the opposite of multiplication. Here is a summary of division equations.
Enjoy the ONE HUNDRED baseballs.

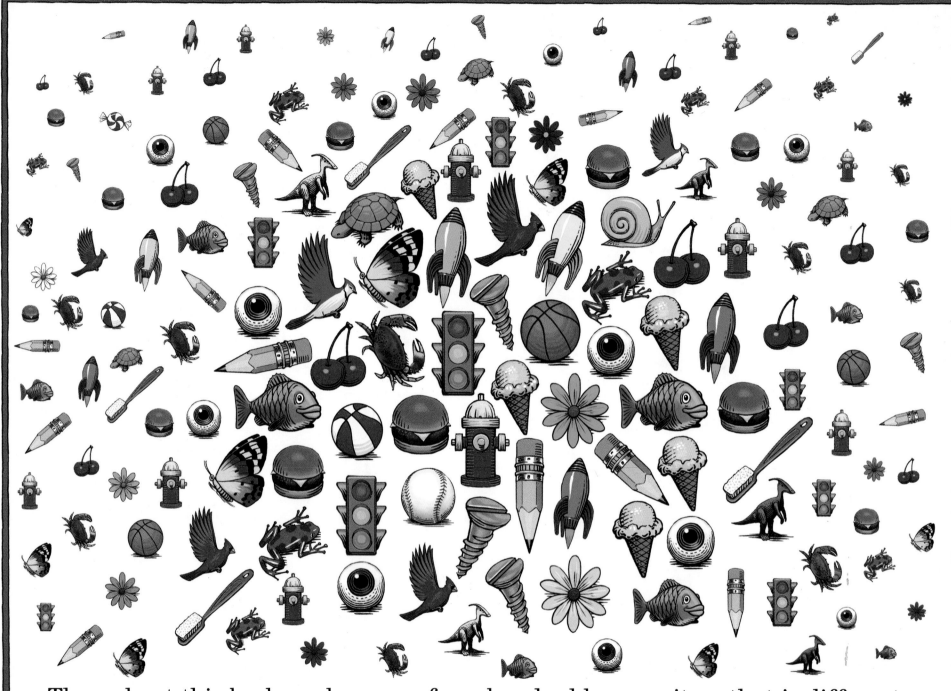

Throughout this book, each group of one hundred has one item that is different.
There are really zillions of ways to count to one hundred.
This book has ended, but using multiplication, addition, subtraction, and division
there is no end to the number of ways you can get to ONE HUNDRED!